Freedom:
Seeing Yourself as God Sees You

A four-week course to help people grow in the
freedom to be themselves.

by
Michael Warden

Apply·It·To·Life™
Adult

BIBLE CURRICULUM
from Group

Group®
Loveland, Colorado

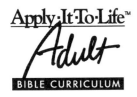

Apply·It·To·Life™
Adult
BIBLE CURRICULUM

Group®

Freedom: Seeing Yourself as God Sees You
Copyright © 1995 Group Publishing, Inc.

Credits
Editors: Stephen Parolini and Bob Buller
Senior Editor: Paul Woods
Creative Products Director: Joani Schultz
Interior Designer: Kathy Benson
Cover Designer: Liz Howe
Cover Illustrator: Thomas Duckworth; The Stock Illustration Source, Inc.
Illustrators: Joel Armstrong and Kathy Benson

ISBN 1-55945-502-0

10 9 8 7 6 5 4 3 2 1   04 03 02 01 00 99 98 97 96 95

Printed in the United States of America.

C O N T E N T S

Introduction

WHAT IS APPLY-IT-TO-LIFE™ ADULT BIBLE CURRICULUM?

Apply-It-To-Life™ Adult Bible Curriculum is a series of four-week study courses designed to help you facilitate powerful lessons that will help class members grow in faith. Use this course with
- Sunday school classes,
- home study groups,
- weekday Bible study groups,
- men's Bible studies,
- women's Bible studies, and
- family classes.

The variety of courses gives the adult student a broad coverage of topical, life-related issues and significant biblical topics. In addition, as the name of the series implies, every lesson helps the adult student apply Scripture to his or her life.

Each course in Apply-It-To-Life Adult Bible Curriculum provides four lessons on different aspects of one topic. In each course, you also receive Fellowship and Outreach Specials connected to the month's topic. They provide suggestions for building closer relationships in your class, outreach activities, and even a party idea!

WHAT MAKES APPLY-IT-TO-LIFE ADULT BIBLE CURRICULUM UNIQUE?

Teaching as Jesus Taught

Jesus was a master teacher. With Apply-It-To-Life Adult Bible Curriculum, you'll use the same teaching methods and principles that Jesus used:

- **Active Learning.** Think back on an important lesson you've learned in life. Did you learn it from reading about it? from hearing about it? from something you did? Chances are, the most important lessons you've learned came from something you experienced. That's what active learning is—learning by doing. Active learning leads students through activities and experiences that help them understand important principles, messages, and ideas. It's a discovery process that helps people internalize and remember what they learn.

Jesus often used active learning. One of the most vivid examples is his washing of his disciples' feet. In Apply-It-To-Life Adult Bible Curriculum, the teacher might remove his or her shoes and socks then read aloud the foot-washing passage from John 13, or the teacher might choose to actually wash people's feet. Participants won't soon forget it. Active learning uses simple activities to teach profound lessons.

● **Interactive Learning.** Interactive learning means learning through small-group interaction and discussion. While it may seem to be a simple concept, it's radically new to many churches that have stuck with a lecture format or large-group discussion for so long. With interactive learning, each person is actively involved in discovering God's truth through talking with other people about God's Word. Interactive learning is discussion with a difference. It puts people in pairs, trios, or foursomes to involve everyone in the learning experience. It takes active learning a step further by having people who have gone through an experience teach others what they've learned.

Jesus often helped cement the learning from an experience by questioning people—sometimes in small groups—about what had happened. He regularly questioned his followers and his opponents, forcing them to think and to discuss among themselves what he was teaching them. After washing his disciples' feet, the first thing Jesus did was ask the disciples if they understood what he had done. After the "foot washing" activity, the teacher might form small groups and have people discuss how they felt when the leader removed his or her shoes and socks. Then group members could compare those feelings and the learning involved to what the disciples must have experienced.

● **Biblical Depth.** Apply-It-To-Life Adult Bible Curriculum recognizes that most adults are ready to go below the surface to better understand the deeper truths of the Bible. Therefore, the activities and studies go beyond an "easy answer" approach to Christian education and lead adults to grapple with difficult issues from a biblical perspective.

Each lesson begins by giving the teacher resource material on the Bible passages covered in the study. In the Bible Basis, you'll find information that will help you understand the Scriptures you're dealing with. Within the class-time section of the lesson, thought-provoking activities and discussions lead adults to new depths of biblical understanding. Bible Insights within the lesson give pertinent information that will bring the Bible to life for you and your class members. In-class handouts give adults significant Bible information and challenge them to search for and discover biblical truths for themselves. Finally, the "For Even Deeper Discussion" sections provide questions that will lead your class members to new and deeper levels of insight and application.

No one questions the depth of Jesus' teachings or the effectiveness of his teaching methods. This curriculum follows Jesus' example and helps people probe the depths of the Bible in a way no other adult curriculum does.

● **Bible Application.** Jesus didn't stop with helping people understand truth. For him, teaching took the learner beyond understanding to application. It wasn't enough that the rich young ruler knew all the right answers. Jesus wanted him to take action on what he knew. In the same way, Apply-It-To-Life Adult Bible Curriculum encourages a response in people's lives. That's why this curriculum is called "Apply-It-To-Life"! Depth of understanding means little if the truths of Scripture don't zing into people's hearts. Each lesson brings home one point and encourages people to consider the changes they might make in response.

● **One Purpose.** In each study, every activity works toward communicating and applying the same point. People may discover other new truths, but the study doesn't load them down with a mass of information. Sometimes less is more. When lessons try to teach too much, they often fail to teach anything. Even Jesus limited his teaching to what he felt people could really learn and apply (John 16:12). Apply-It-To-Life Adult Bible Curriculum makes sure that class members thoroughly understand and apply one point each week.

● **Variety.** People appreciate variety. Jesus constantly varied his teaching methods. One day he would have a serious discussion with his disciples about who he was and another day he'd baffle them by turning water into wine. What he didn't do was allow them to become bored with what he had to teach them.

Any kind of study can become less than exciting if the leader and students do everything the same way week after week. Apply-It-To-Life Adult Bible Curriculum varies activities and approaches to keep everyone's interest level high each week. In one class, you might have people in small groups "put themselves in the disciples' sandals" and experience something of the confusion of Jesus' death and resurrection. In another lesson, class members may experience problems in communication and examine how such problems can damage relationships.

To meet adults' varied needs, the courses cover a wide range of topics such as Jesus, knowing God's will, communication, taking faith to work, and highlights of Bible books. One month you may choose to study a family or personal faith issue; the next month you may cover a biblical topic such as the book of John.

● **Relevance.** People today want to know how to live successfully right now. They struggle with living as authentic Christians at work, in the family, and in the community. Most churchgoing adults want to learn about the Bible, but not merely for the sake of having greater Bible knowledge. They want to know how the Bible can help them live faithful lives—how it can help them face the difficulties of living in today's culture. Apply-It-To-Life Adult Bible Curriculum bridges the gap between biblical truth and the "real world" issues of people's lives. Jesus didn't discuss with his followers the eschatological significance of Ezekiel's wheels, and Apply-It-To-Life Bible Curriculum won't either! Courses and studies in this curriculum focus on the real needs of people and help them discover answers in Scripture that will help meet those needs.

● **A Nonthreatening Atmosphere.** In many adult classes, people feel intimidated because they're new Christians or because they don't have the Bible knowledge they think they should have. Jesus sometimes intimidated those who opposed him, but he consistently treated his followers with understanding and respect. We want people in church to experience the same understanding and respect Jesus' followers experienced. With Apply-It-To-Life Adult Bible Curriculum, no one is embarrassed for not knowing or understanding as much as someone else. In fact, the interactive learning process minimizes the differences between those with vast Bible knowledge and those with little Bible knowledge. Lessons often begin with nonthreatening, sharing questions and move slowly toward more depth. Whatever their level of knowledge or commitment, class members will work together to discover biblical truths that can affect their lives.

● **A Group That Cares.** Jesus began his ministry by choosing a group of 12 people who learned from him together. That group practically lived together—sharing one another's hurts, joys, and ambitions. Sometimes Jesus divided the 12 into smaller groups and worked with just three or four at a time.

Studies have shown that many adults today long for a close-knit group of people with whom they can share personal needs and joys. And people interact more freely when they feel accepted in a group. Activities in this curriculum will help class members get to know one another better and care for one another more as they study the Bible and apply its truths to their lives. As people reveal their thoughts and feelings to one another, they'll grow closer and develop more commitment to the group and to each other. And they'll be encouraging one another along the way!

● **An Element of Delight.** We don't often think about Jesus' ministry in this way, but there certainly were times he brought fun and delight to his followers. Remember the time he raised Peter's mother-in-law? or the time he sat happily with children on his lap? How about the joy and excitement at his triumphal entry into Jerusalem? or the time he helped fishing disciples catch a boatload of fish—after they'd fished all night with no success?

People learn more when they're having fun. So within Apply-It-To-Life Adult Bible Curriculum, elements of fun and delight pop up often. And sometimes adding fun is as simple as using a carrot for a pretend microphone!

Taking the Fear Out of Teaching

Teachers love Apply-It-To-Life Adult Bible Curriculum because it makes teaching much less stressful. Lessons in this curriculum

● **are easy to teach.** Interactive learning frees the teacher from being a dispenser of information to serve as a facilitator of learning. Teachers can spend class time guiding people to discover and apply biblical truths. The studies provide clear, understandable Bible background; easy-to-prepare learning experiences; and powerful, thought-provoking discussion questions.

● **can be prepared quickly.** Lessons in Apply-It-To-Life Adult Bible Curriculum are logical and clear. There's no sorting through tons of information to figure out the lesson. In 30 minutes, a busy teacher can easily read a lesson and prepare to teach it. In addition, optional and For Extra Time activities allow the teacher to tailor the lesson to the class. and the thorough instructions and questions will guide even an inexperienced teacher through each powerful lesson.

● **let everyone share in the class's success.** With Apply-It-To-Life Adult Bible Curriculum, the teacher is one of the participants. The teacher still guides the class, but the burden is not as heavy. Everyone participates and adds to the study's effectiveness. So when the study has an impact, everyone shares in that success.

● **lead the teacher to new discoveries.** Each lesson is designed to help the teacher first discover a biblical truth. And most teachers will make additional discoveries as they prepare each lesson. In class, the teacher will discover even more as other adults share what they have found. As with any type of teaching, the teacher will likely learn more than anyone else in the class!

● **provide relevant information to class members.**

Photocopiable handouts are designed to help people better understand or interpret Bible passages. And the handouts make teaching easier because the teacher can often refer to them for small-group discussion questions and instructions.

First familiarize yourself with an Apply-It-To-Life Adult Bible Curriculum lesson. The following explanations will help you understand how the lesson elements work together.

Lesson Elements

● The **Opening** maps out the lesson's agenda and introduces your class to the topic for the session. Sometimes this activity will help people get better acquainted as they begin to explore the topic together.

● The **Bible Exploration and Application** activities will help people discover what the Bible says about the topic and how the lesson's point applies to their lives. In these varied activities, class members find answers to the "So what?" question. Through active and interactive learning methods, people will discover the relevance of the Scriptures and commit to growing closer to God.

You may use either one or both of the options in this section. They are designed to stand alone or to work together. Both present the same point in different ways. "For Even Deeper Discussion" questions appear at the end of each activity in this section. Use these questions whenever you feel they might be particularly helpful for your class.

● The **Closing** pulls everything in the lesson together and often funnels the lesson's message into a time of reflection and prayer.

● The **For Extra Time** section is just that. Use it when you've completed the lesson and still have time left or when you've used one Bible Exploration and Application option and don't have time to do the other. Or you might plan to use it instead of another option.

When you put all the sections together, you get a lesson that's fun and easy to teach. Plus, participants will learn truths they'll remember and apply to their daily lives.

About the Questions and Answers

The answers given after discussion questions are responses participants *might* give. They aren't the only answers or the "right" answers. However, you can use them to spark discussion.

Real life doesn't always allow us to give the "right" answers. That's why some of the responses given are negative or controversial. If someone responds negatively, don't be shocked. Accept the person and use the opportunity to explore other perspectives on the issue.

To get more out of your discussions, use follow-up inquiries such as

- Tell me more.
- What do you mean by that?
- What makes you feel that way?

Guidelines for a Successful Adult Class

- **Be a facilitator, not a lecturer.** Apply-It-To-Life Adult Bible Curriculum is student-based rather than teacher-based. Your job is to direct the activities and facilitate the discussions. You become a choreographer of sorts: someone who gets everyone else involved in the discussion and keeps the discussion on track.

- **Teach adults how to form small groups.** Help adults discover the benefits of small-group discussions by assisting them in forming groups of four, three, or two—whatever the activity calls for. Small-group sharing allows for more discussion and involvement by all participants. It's not as threatening or scary to open up to two people as it would be to 20 or 200!

Some leaders decide not to form small groups because they want to hear everybody's ideas. The intention is good, but some people just won't talk in a large group. Use a "report back" time after small-group discussions to gather the best responses from all groups.

When you form small groups, don't always let people choose those right around them. Try creative group-forming methods to help everyone in the class get to know one another. For example, tell class members: find three other people wearing the same color you are; join two other people who like the same music you do; locate three others who shop at the same grocery store you do; find one who was born the same month as you; choose three who like the same season as you, and so on. If you have fun with it, your class will, too!

● **Encourage relationship building.** George Barna, in his insightful book about the church, *The Frog in the Kettle,* explains that adults today have a strong need to develop friendships. In a society of high-tech toys, "personal" computers, and lonely commutes, people long for positive human contact. That's where our church classes and groups can jump in. Help adults form friendships through your class. What's discovered in a classroom setting will be better applied when friends support each other outside the classroom. In fact, the relationships begun in your class may be as important as the truths you help your adults learn.

● **Be flexible.** Sometimes your class will complete every activity in the lesson with great success and wonderful learning. But what should you do if people go off on a tangent? or they get stuck in one of the activities? What if you don't have time to finish the lesson?

Don't panic. People learn best when they are interested and engaged in meaningful discussion, when they move at their own pace. And if you get through even one activity, your class will discover the point for the whole lesson. So relax. It's OK if you don't get everything done. Try to get to the Closing in every lesson, since its purpose is to bring closure to the topic for the week. But if you don't, don't sweat it!

● **Expect the unexpected.** Active learning is an adventure that doesn't always take you where you think you're going. Don't be surprised if things don't go exactly the way you'd planned. Be open to the different directions the Holy Spirit may lead your class. When something goes wrong or an unexpected emotion is aroused, take advantage of this teachable moment. Ask probing questions; follow up on someone's deep need or concern. Those moments are often the best opportunities for learning that come our way.

● **Participate—and encourage participation.** Apply-It-To-Life Adult Bible Curriculum is only as interactive as you and your class make it. Learning arises out of dialogue. People need to grapple with and verbalize their questions and discoveries. Jump into discussions yourself, but don't "take over." Encourage everyone to participate. You can facilitate smooth discussions by using "active listening" responses such as rephrasing and summing up what's been said. If people seem stumped, use the possible responses after each question to spark further discussion. You may feel like a cheerleader at times, but your efforts will be worth it. The more people participate, the more they'll discover God's truths for themselves.

● **Trust the Holy Spirit.** All the previous six guidelines and the instructions in the lessons will be irrelevant if you ignore the presence of God in your classroom. God sent the Holy Spirit as our helper. As you use this curriculum, ask the Holy Spirit to help you facilitate the lessons. And ask the Holy Spirit to direct your class toward God's truth. Trust that God's Spirit can work through each person's discoveries, not just the teacher's.

How to Use This Course

Before the Four-Week Session
- Read the Course Introduction and This Course at a Glance (pp. 13-15).
- Decide how you'll use the art on the Publicity Page (p. 16) to publicize the course. Prepare fliers, newsletter articles, and posters as needed.
- Look at the Fellowship and Outreach Specials (pp. 63-64) and decide which ones you'll use.

Before Each Lesson
- Read the one-sentence Point, the Objectives, and the Bible Basis for the lesson. The Bible Basis provides background information on the lesson's passages and shows how those passages relate to people today.
- Choose which activities you'll use from the lesson. Remember, it's not important to do every activity. Pick the ones that best fit your group and time allotment.
- Gather necessary supplies. They're listed in This Lesson at a Glance.
- Read each section of the lesson. Adjust activities as necessary to fit your class size and meeting room, but be careful not to delete all the activity. People learn best when they're actively involved in the learning process.

COURSE INTRODUCTION— FREEDOM: SEEING YOURSELF AS GOD SEES YOU

Imagine that you're an architect building your dream house. You draw up the plans with exacting detail and meticulous care. You choose only the best materials and provide for a strong foundation. Only when you're convinced that every detail is perfect do you hand your blueprint over to the builders to create your masterpiece.

But then something terrible happens. When the builders begin work on your dream house, they toss the blueprint aside and build whatever they see fit. Each builder follows his or her own ideas. They don't listen to one another and certainly not to you. In the end, even though your dream house was created out of the supplies you provided, it doesn't look anything like what you had envisioned. In fact, some parts of it don't look like much of anything.

How would you feel?

Well, that's exactly how God often feels about us, his children. God is the architect of our souls. He knows who we are (and who we are *not*) better than anyone. But in the course of our lives, his plans often get distorted. We form beliefs, attitudes, and fears that God never intended. By the time we're "grown up," we may not look anything like what God intended for us. As a result, we have only a vague idea of our own identity, and very little in life is particularly fulfilling. Like a structure with no unified design or purpose, we constantly wonder who we are and what we're made for.

This course is all about rebuilding people's lives according to God's original blueprint. During the four weeks of this course, participants will be asked to take a critical look at their lives—what they believe about God, themselves, and the world around them—and compare those beliefs with the truths found in God's Word. They'll learn how to tear down any "false structures" in their lives and to rebuild their identities according to God's truth. They'll also learn how to set a course for the future that will help them stay on the right track from this point onward.

Can all that be accomplished in four weeks? Probably not. People are not machines in which defective parts can be easily repaired or replaced. For this reason, the course isn't structured to totally redesign people in four weeks' time. Rather, the course focuses on giving your class members the information and tools they need to seek out and find answers on their own. Building an accurate and healthy self-identity may take months or years, but this course provides an excellent starting place. With God's help, your adults will be able to move beyond this experience to live extraordinary lives.

This Course at a Glance

Before you dive into the lessons, familiarize yourself with each lesson's point. Then read the Scripture passages.

● Study them as a background to the lessons.
● Use them as a basis for your personal devotions.
● Think about how they relate to adults' circumstances today.

Lesson 1: The Making of Me

The Point: Our self-concept stems largely from childhood experiences.

Bible Basis: Genesis 25:19-34; 27:5-29; 1 Samuel 3:1–4:1a; 8:1-9; 12:1-5; and Philippians 3:4b-21

Lesson 2: Living the Lies

The Point: Lies we believe about ourselves influence the way we live our lives.

Bible Basis: 1 Samuel 9:25–10:1, 14-24; 15:1-26; and Philippians 4:8

Lesson 3: Who Am I, Really?

The Point: Our true identities are found only in Christ.

Bible Basis: Romans 8:31-39 and Ephesians 2:1-10

Lesson 4: From Here to Eternity

The Point: With God's help, we can live fulfilled, purposeful lives.

Bible Basis: Philippians 3:7-14 and 2 Timothy 4:6-8

Grab your congregation's attention! Add the vital details to the ready-made flier below, photocopy it, and use it to advertise this course on your identity in Christ. Insert the flier in your bulletins. Enlarge it to make posters. Splash the art or anything else from this page in newsletters, bulletins, or even on postcards! It's that simple.

*The art from this page is also available on Group's MinistryNet™ computer on-line resource for you to manipulate on your computer. Call **800-447-1070** for information.*

A four-week adult course on discovering who you really are.

COME TO

ON

AT

FREEDOM:
SEEING YOURSELF
AS GOD SEES YOU

COME EXPLORE HOW YOU CAN FULFILL YOUR TRUE POTENTIAL!

Apply·It·To·Life™
Adult
BIBLE CURRICULUM
from Group

FREEDOM:
SEEING YOURSELF
AS GOD SEES YOU

FREEDOM:
SEEING YOURSELF
AS GOD SEES YOU

FREEDOM:
SEEING YOURSELF
AS GOD SEES YOU

FREEDOM:
SEEING YOURSELF
AS GOD SEES YOU

The Making of Me

Our self-concept stems largely from childhood experiences.

◀ THE POINT

OBJECTIVES

Participants will
- learn how childhood experiences shape a person's self-image,
- explore how their own self-images were shaped,
- identify areas in which they would like to change, and
- commit to condfidentiality throughout the course.

BIBLE BASIS

Look up the Scriptures. Then read the following paragraphs to see how the passages relate to people today.

Genesis 25:19-34 and **27:5-29** describe the conflicts between Jacob and Esau.

GENESIS 25:19-34; 27:5-29

Sibling relationships are often difficult. That between Jacob and Esau was no different. These twins waged a life-long battle for a variety of things, including the love and favor of their parents—Isaac and Rebekah—and control of the family fortune. However, in spite of (and even through) this conflict, God worked to maintain his promise to Abraham (Genesis 12:1-3; 17:1-8).

The story begins with a threat to the promise: Rebekah, like her mother-in-law, Sarah, was childless for many years (Genesis 16:1). But when Isaac prayed to God on Rebekah's behalf, God intervened, and she conceived twins. But the two children struggled within her womb, so Rebekah asked God to explain what it meant. God's answer was surprising: Contrary to the social practices of that day, the elder (Esau) would serve the younger (Jacob).

This revelation was certain to create conflicts, and Rebekah's preference for Jacob and Isaac's partiality toward Esau only intensified the animosity. But God's announcement should have given Jacob the confidence to wait for God's intervention. It didn't. Genesis 25:29-34 reports that Jacob took advantage of Esau's hunger and secured Esau's right to inherit the family property. Also, Genesis 27:1-45 describes how Rebekah and Jacob tricked Isaac into giving Jacob the blessing meant for Esau.

Jacob is never condemned for his opportunism and deceit. Still, he is also never praised, and he could have avoided many battles by following his parents' example of praying for divine intervention and guidance. Unfortunately, Jacob seems to have been so insecure that he resorted to trickery and deception to gain what he wanted.

1 SAMUEL 3:1–4:1; 8:1-9; 12:1-5

1 Samuel 3:1–4:1a; 8:1-9; and **12:1-5** tell about the beginning and end of Samuel's ministry.

Like Jacob, Samuel was a child of promise. Hannah, his mother, had asked God for a son, and God had given her Samuel (1 Samuel 1:1-20). However, unlike Jacob, Samuel's life reflected the clarity of purpose and confidence of someone who clearly understood who he was in God's eyes.

In all likelihood, Samuel's childhood experiences produced this positive self-image. Hannah dedicated Samuel to the Lord and sent him to serve in the temple of the Lord at Shiloh (1 Samuel 1:21-28). As a result, Samuel formed his identity primarily in relation to God and not in rivalry with others. Then, when Samuel was still young, God spoke directly to him one night. The message of judgment against the priest Eli certainly reinforced Samuel's sense of calling and his commitment to serve God.

Since Samuel knew who he was, he was able to accept Israel's demand for a king. The people were rejecting God, not him. Moreover, at the end of his life Samuel was able to claim that he had never defrauded or taken advantage of anyone. Samuel was, in sum, a perfect example of someone who understood who he was as a child of promise.

PHILIPPIANS 3:4b-21

Philippians 3:4b-21 records Paul's description of his early life as a devoted Jew and his later opinion of that life.

Sometimes even a largely accurate self-image can mislead a person. Such was the case with Paul. Before he became a Christian, he regarded himself a devout man, a protector of the faith. There was only one problem. Paul's faith was in his own ability to obey the Law and not in Christ. So all of his credentials as a pillar of the Jewish faith really amounted to nothing.

But that didn't mean that Paul had to completely re-create his self-identity when he became a Christian. He simply needed to make sure that his faith was only in Christ. When Paul realized who he was in Christ, the rest of his life came into focus. He saw that what really mattered was knowing and serving Christ.

Paul's redirected self-image later enabled him to evaluate his situation accurately. He knew that he was on a journey but had not yet reached his goal. However, he also saw the progress he had made. In fact, he was so confident in his new identity and life in Christ that he held himself up as an example for others to follow. With a clear understanding of who he was, Paul was able to achieve his full potential as a child and servant of God.

These passages illustrate an important principle: People shape their lives according to what they believe about themselves. This lesson will help people begin to discover their true identities as Christians and as humans created in God's image by showing them how childhood experiences have affected how they see themselves.

THIS LESSON AT A GLANCE

Section	Minutes	What Participants Will Do	Supplies
OPENING	*up to 10*	**GETTING TO KNOW ME**—Describe themselves as if they're talking to people they don't know.	
BIBLE EXPLORATION AND APPLICATION	*20 to 30*	☐ *Option 1:* **THE MAKING OF ME**—Create crooked time lines of their lives, then examine how Jacob's and Samuel's childhood experiences shaped their lives.	Bibles, newsprint, markers, "Trickster or Prophet" handouts (p. 26)
	15 to 20	☐ *Option 2:* **WHAT I THINK ABOUT ME**—Discuss Philippians 3:4b-21, then create personality profiles of themselves.	Bibles, pencils, "What I Think About Me" handouts (p. 27)
CLOSING	*up to 5*	**ONE THING I'D CHANGE**—Name one thing about themselves they'd like to change, then commit themselves to each other in prayer.	
FOR EXTRA TIME	*up to 10*	**MY MOST EMBARRASSING MOMENT**—Tell their most embarrassing moments.	
	up to 10	**TEST RESULTS**—Discuss how personality tests have helped them understand themselves.	

Getting to Know Me
(up to 10 minutes)

As you begin the class, tell adults what you'll be learning in today's lesson. Use the following statement or your own summary of the main point: **Welcome to the first of four classes on the topic of self-identity. In this study, we're going to discover who we really are as individuals in Christ, then uncover the hindrances that keep us from reaching our true potential.**  **We'll start today by exploring how our self-concepts stem largely from childhood experiences.**

Open with prayer, then form circles of no more than six. Say: **Before we talk about our true identities in Christ, let's learn about how we see ourselves. As we go around the circle, I want each of you to say how you'd describe yourself to someone who didn't know you. There's only one rule—no modesty!**

Go around the circle and let each person share. After each person shares, encourage him or her to explain the description by asking follow-up questions such as:

● **Why did you describe yourself in terms of your** (job, family role, faith in God, or hobbies)**?**
● **Why did you focus on the qualities you did?**
● **Why do you find it difficult to describe yourself?**

After everyone has shared, say: **Whether or not we know it, all of us have "blueprints" in our minds that tell us who we are. Some people's blueprints are accurate, but other people have blueprints that are way off the mark.** ▶ **Whether it's right or wrong, your self-concept stems largely from your childhood experiences. Today we're going to explore how that blueprint process works.**

THE POINT ▶

TEACHER TIP
Encourage class members to speak as freely as they're able. Make sure they understand that there are no stupid ideas or comments. Encourage everyone to work together as people on a united adventure, so they'll feel free to relax and share from the heart.

THE POINT ▶

☐ **OPTION 1:**
The Making of Me
(20 to 30 minutes)

Before class, photocopy and cut apart the "Trickster or Prophet" handout (p. 26). You'll need one photocopy for every two adults.

Give each class member a sheet of newsprint and a marker. Have each person draw on the newsprint a large time line of his or her life from birth to the present.

TEACHER TIP
If you don't have access to newsprint, you can use regular sheets of paper instead.

Instruct people to note on their time lines major events and times when specific people or groups strongly influenced or changed them in some way. Encourage everyone to mark both positive and negative influences.

Tell everyone to emphasize the formative events and influential people by changing the direction of the time line either up or down whenever they appear. As a result, adults should end up with zigzag time lines.

When everyone is finished, have class members display and explain their time lines, with special emphasis on the major turning points in their lives. After everyone has shared, form groups of four and have groups discuss the following questions. Ask:

● **Which event or person had the most positive effect on you? Explain.** (My sister took me along whenever she went out with her friends; my dad took me to swim lessons every Saturday for two months.)

● **Which event or person had the most negative effect on you? Explain.** (My parents divorced when I was 12, and I didn't see my dad much after that; my English teacher called me stupid in front of the class.)

● **What's your reaction to having such an erratic time line?** (I feel embarrassed about all the stuff that has gone on in my life; I can see how the person I've become has been shaped by a variety of influences.)

● **How is the shape of your time line like the way you sometimes see yourself?** (I've been shaped by many things, so it's hard to come up with a simple, unified picture of who I am; I often see myself as going off in a thousand directions at once, just like my time line.)

● **How do major events and important people shape our beliefs about ourselves?** (We believe what others say about us, especially if those people are important to us; I think the way we react to major events shapes our identities more than the events themselves.)

● **In your own life, which time period and which people were most influential in shaping the way you see yourself?** (During my childhood—my parents; the last year and a half—my spouse and kids.)

Say: **Influential times and significant people will continue to shape our identities the rest of our lives.** ▶ **But generally a person's foundational self-identity stems largely from childhood experiences. For most of us, these formative experiences took place in the home. Those events and people told us who we were, and, to a large extent, we still carry those identities with us. Let's look at several biblical examples of what we've been talking about.**

◀ T H E   P O I N T

Tell people to stay in their foursomes and number off

BIBLE INSIGHT

Conflict marked Jacob's entire life. He tussled with his father-in-law, Laban, on several occasions (Genesis 29:14b-28; 30:25-43; 31:1-54). In addition, when Jacob returned to Canaan he wrestled with God (Genesis 32:1-32). Finally, it appears that Jacob deceived Esau even as he claimed to be making peace with him. That is, Jacob told Esau he'd follow him south to Seir, but he actually went west to Succoth and settled near Shechem (Genesis 33:12-18). It's hardly surprising that Jacob's sons continued his dubious heritage (Genesis 34:1-31; 37:1-36).

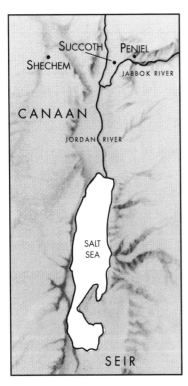

from one to four. Have the ones gather in one area, the twos in another, and so on. Give a copy of the top half of the "Trickster or Prophet" handout to each person in the ones and twos and a copy of the bottom half to each person in the threes and fours.

Instruct groups to read and follow the handout instructions. After about 10 minutes, have people return to their original foursomes and share any insights with other group members. After several minutes, ask class members to discuss the following questions in their groups. Ask:

● **Which of the two biblical characters do you most closely identify with? Why?** (Jacob, because my father liked my brother more than me; Jacob, because I've always competed with my sister; Samuel, because my parents viewed me as a gift from God.)

● **How were your childhood experiences like those characters' experiences? How were they different?** (I grew up surrounded by a lot of conflict; my parents had a lot of expectations about me; I was taught always to put God first.)

● **How can you avoid acting like Jacob?** (I can remind myself that God loves me as much as he loves anyone else; I can make peace with my brother; I can recognize why I'm always competing against others.)

● **How can you be more like Samuel?** (I can put God's interests first; I can be accountable to others; I can realize that I'm a special child of God.)

Say: **It's true that ▶ our self-concept stems largely from our childhood experiences, but that doesn't mean that we can't change how we view ourselves. It does mean that we must begin by examining our self-image and understanding how it was formed. Only then will we be ready to develop a healthy and positive self-identity of who we are in Jesus Christ.**

■ ■

FOR *Even Deeper* **DISCUSSION**

● To what extent did Jacob respond to his destiny (see Genesis 25:23) correctly? How might he have responded more appropriately?

● What do you think is your destiny? How does it shape your self-image? your behavior?

■ ■

□ OPTION 2:
What I Think About Me
(15 to 20 minutes)

Before class, make one copy of the "What I Think About Me" handout (p. 27) for each person.

Have class members form pairs. Say: **Let's take a moment to look at the experiences that shaped the Apostle Paul and how he evaluated those experiences. In your pairs, read Philippians 3:4b-6, then discuss the following questions in your pairs.** Ask:

● **What was Paul's self-image before he became a Christian?** (He thought that he was very righteous; he defined himself in terms of the Law.)

● **To what extent was that self-image accurate?** (He wasn't really righteous; he was a very devout person; his commitment was misguided but sincere.)

Say: **Now read Philippians 3:7-21 and answer these questions.** Ask:

● **How much did Paul's self-image change when he became a Christian? How much did it remain the same?** (He measured himself against Jesus instead of the Law; he remained a very devout person.)

● **How did Paul redirect his basic view of himself when he became a Christian?** (He was just as devoted to Jesus as he had been to the Law; the object of his faith changed, but he was still a defender of the faith; he used his earlier experiences to show others their need for Christ.)

Have partners share each other's insights with the whole class. Then ask:

● **What can we learn from Paul's experiences?** (Our self-image may be fairly accurate but misdirected; we may have a faulty self-identity because we're measuring ourselves against the wrong thing; it's possible to make significant changes even late in life.)

● **What happens when people "buy into" a set of wrong beliefs about themselves?** (They live according to what they believe; they're never happy in life but may not be sure why; they damage themselves and others.)

● **What happens when people see themselves as God sees them?** (They learn to accept themselves; they see their strengths and their weaknesses; they begin to understand how to be content.)

● **Why do you think childhood experiences are so influential?** (We see ourselves as our parents see us; first impressions are hard to change, even when they're of ourselves.)

Say: ▶ **Now that we've seen how our self-concept stems largely from childhood, let's see if we can describe exactly how we see ourselves.**

TEACHER **TIP**

To make it easier for pairs to remember the questions, hang a sheet of newsprint at the front of the room and write the questions on it.

◀ THE POINT

TEACHER
TIP

Encourage participants to relax and be honest as they write. Remind them that the whole class is going through this journey of self-discovery together, so it's important to trust one another.

Give each person a copy of the "What I Think About Me" handout and a pencil. Instruct class members to use their handouts to write personality profiles of themselves, which they will share with their partners.

Once everyone has completed the handout, have partners share what they wrote with each other. Then call everyone together and ask:

● **How did it feel to talk about your self-image?** (It felt good because I'm proud of who I am; I'm shy, so I felt uncomfortable; it was painful to relive my struggles.)

● **Why is sharing about who you are such a vulnerable thing to do?** (I'm afraid others will reject me; it forces me to be honest with myself.)

● **Why is it important to talk about who you think you are with others?** (Because they can give you an outside perspective; because it's an important step toward realizing you're acceptable, warts and all; because it forces you to put your feelings into words.)

Say: **Let's close today by learning to trust each other a little more.**

■■■■■■■■■■■■■■■■■■■■■■■■■■■■■■■

For *Even Deeper*
DISCUSSION

● According to Philippians 3:12-14, what is Paul's goal? How does forgetting what is behind and straining toward what is ahead affect your self-image?

● Read Proverbs 22:6. How does this verse apply to helping children develop healthy self-images? What might be the consequences of giving a child a negative or inaccurate self-image?

■■■■■■■■■■■■■■■■■■■■■■■■■■■■■■■

APPLY▪IT▪TO
LIFE
T·H·IS   WEEK

The "Apply-It-To-Life This Week" handout (p. 28) helps people further explore the issues uncovered in today's class. Give everyone a photocopy of the handout. Encourage class members to take time during the coming week to explore the questions and activities listed on the handout.

TEACHER
TIP

The Closing activity works best with groups of eight or fewer.

CLOSING

One Thing I'd Change
(up to 5 minutes)

Form a circle. Have class members take turns

telling one thing they'd like to change about themselves. For example, someone might say, "I wish I was better at getting places on time" or "I'd like to be more tolerant." After each person shares, have two volunteers each tell one way that person should never change. For example, someone might say, "You should never change the way you smile when you walk into a room" or "You should never change the way you always help people."

After everyone has shared, say: **During the next three weeks, we're going to examine what we think of ourselves and discover the identities God created us to have. As we close in prayer today, let's commit to keeping what's been discussed in confidence.**

Close with prayer, asking God to protect everyone's dignity and to guide class members to a deeper understanding of themselves.

 For Extra Time

MY MOST EMBARRASSING MOMENT

(up to 10 minutes)

As a way to help class members become more comfortable with each other, have them describe their most embarrassing moments. For fun, keep track of the stories and award prizes that reflect the uniqueness of the stories. For example, give a Baby Ruth candy bar to the person with the "nuttiest" anecdote.

TEST RESULTS

(up to 10 minutes)

Ask if anyone in the class has ever taken a personality test, such as the Myers-Briggs test, the DISC test, or another like it. Ask people who have taken one of these tests to describe their experiences. Then have the entire class discuss the following questions. Ask:

● **What are the strengths of tests like these? What are the weaknesses?**

● **How much should we rely on the conclusions of these tests?**

● **What part should Scripture play in self-evaluation?**

● **What role should the Holy Spirit play in self-evaluation?**

■ Trickster or Prophet

■ THE TRICKSTER

When it became apparent that Rebekah couldn't have children, Isaac prayed to God. God answered his prayer, and Rebekah became pregnant with twins. However, God also told Rebekah that, contrary to the normal practices of that day, the older son (Esau) would serve the younger (Jacob).

- Read Genesis 25:19-28. How would you expect Jacob's self-image to be influenced by the fact that he had a twin brother? by the expectations associated with his birth? by his father's preference for Esau? by his mother's preference for him?

- Read Genesis 25:29-34. What does this passage reveal about Jacob's self-image?

- How do you think Jacob's childhood experiences contributed to this self-image?

- Read Genesis 27:5-29. How is Jacob's self-image the same as it was in 25:29-34? How is it different?

- How are Jacob's childhood experiences reflected in his self-image?

■ THE PROPHET

God answered Hannah's prayer for a son, so Hannah gave her son (Samuel) back to the Lord (1 Samuel 1:24-28). When she had weaned Samuel, Hannah took him to the temple at Shiloh. From that day on, Samuel lived at the temple and helped Eli the priest with the temple services. God first spoke to Samuel while Samuel was at Shiloh.

- Read 1 Samuel 3:1–4:1a. How would you expect Samuel's self-image to be influenced by the fact that he was an answer to prayer? by being raised at the temple? by the revelation of judgment against Eli? by his recognition as a prophet?

- Read 1 Samuel 8:1-9. What does this passage reveal about Samuel's self-image?

- How do you think Samuel's childhood experiences contributed to this self-image?

- Read 1 Samuel 12:1-5. How is Samuel's self-image the same as it was in 8:1-9? How is it different?

- How are Samuel's childhood experiences reflected in this self-image?

■ What I Think About Me

Create a personality profile of yourself by supplying the information requested for each category. Answer as honestly as you can. You'll be sharing your answers with your partner in several minutes.

My name:

My parents' names:

Three adjectives I'd use to describe myself:

One thing my mother taught me:

One thing my father taught me:

My two greatest weaknesses as a person:

My two greatest strengths as a person:

My two most important goals in life:

The toughest part of my faith journey:

The best thing about being a Christian:

One thing from my past I wish I could forget:

The Making of Me

The Point: ▶ Our self-concept stems largely from childhood experiences.
Scripture Focus: Genesis 25:19-34; 27:5-29; 1 Samuel 3:1–4:1a; 8:1-9; 12:1-5; and Philippians 3:4b-21

Reflecting on God's Word

Each day this week, read one of the following Scriptures and examine how someone's beliefs can affect the kind of person he or she becomes. Then apply your insights to your own life. You may want to list your discoveries in the space under each passage.

Day 1: 1 Samuel 10:17-24; 15:1-35. Saul gains, then loses the kingship.

Day 2: 2 Corinthians 2:12–3:6. Paul's confidence comes from Christ.

Day 3: Psalm 23:1-6. David expresses his confidence in God.

Day 4: 2 Thessalonians 2:9-12. Hating the truth brings condemnation.

Day 5: Jonah 3:3-10. The king of Nineveh repents from his sin.

Day 6: John 17:1-5. Jesus approaches the cross confidently.

Beyond Reflection

1. Contact one or more significant people from your past or present and ask them to respond to this question: "How would you describe me to someone who didn't know me?" Keep notes of what each person says, then combine the information to see if you can find patterns that might help you gain a deeper understanding of yourself.

2. As a way to clarify how you see yourself, consider taking one of the standard personality tests available today. The Myers-Briggs and the DISC tests are both easy to take and understand and can provide helpful information in understanding your self-image.

3. Think of someone you've known from childhood. For example, you might want to think of a brother, sister, cousin, or close friend. Then answer these questions:
  ● How was that person's self-identity shaped by his or her childhood experiences?
  ● How have you been shaped by the same or similar childhood experiences?
  ● How have you reacted differently to the same experiences?
  ● What do your reactions reveal about yourself? about your self-identity?

Next Week's Bible Passages: 1 Samuel 9:25–10:1, 14-24; 15:1-26; and Philippians 4:8

Living the Lies

Lies we believe about ourselves influence the way we live our lives.

◀ T H E   P O I N T

OBJECTIVES

Participants will
● discuss the power of words to hurt and to heal,
● discover how inaccurate self-images are formed,
● explore how their self-images influence their actions, and
● thank God for the positive qualities he has given them.

BIBLE BASIS

Look up the following Scriptures. Then read the following background sections to see how the passages relate to people today.

In **1 Samuel 9:25–10:1; 10:14-24;** and **15:1-26** Saul gains, then loses a kingdom.

Saul had every reason to succeed. He was God's first choice to be Israel's first king. Moreover, he had been filled with God's Spirit and thus equipped to rule as God wanted (1 Samuel 10:9-11). Finally, since Saul was taller than every other Israelite, he even had the look and the stature of a king. In spite of all that, Saul failed miserably, a victim of his own insecurities and disobedience.

Part of Saul's problem may have been that he never expected to become king. One day he went looking for lost donkeys; he had no idea he would find a kingdom instead (1 Samuel 9:1-17). But Saul should have known when Samuel anointed his head with oil that he alone was God's chosen king. He also should have acted with the confidence that befits a king. Unfortunately, Saul shrank from his task from the very beginning.

1 SAMUEL 9:25–10:1;
10:14-24;
15:1-26

In the first place, Saul hid the fact that Samuel had anointed him king. Then, when Samuel tried to present Saul to the Israelites, God had to tell Samuel where to find the new king. Saul was hiding among the baggage—Israel's leader was too shy to appear before his people. During the years that followed, it became apparent that Saul was also too afraid to lead the people.

The clearest example of Saul's fear is described in 1 Samuel 15. God, through his prophet Samuel, commanded Saul to punish the Amalekites for their earlier hostilities against Israel. Saul was to completely destroy the Amalekites and their possessions. For the most part, Saul obeyed. However, he *and the people* spared Agag, the Amalekite king, and the best of the livestock (1 Samuel 15:9, 15).

When Samuel confronted Saul for his partial obedience, Saul first explained that the livestock had been saved to sacrifice to the Lord. Then Saul claimed that he had done everything God had ordered but that the people had disobeyed God (1 Samuel 15:20-21). Samuel wasn't convinced. He knew that Saul was at fault. He also recognized that Saul had never seen himself as God saw him, as king. Eventually Saul agreed: He had sinned because he was afraid of the people.

Like Saul, many people today fail to live up to their potential because they see themselves as inadequate. They seem to think that God will ask more of them than they can possibly deliver. We all need to understand that God always enables us to become the people he wants us to be. In many cases, we simply need to see ourselves as God sees us.

PHILIPPIANS 4:8

In **Philippians 4:8,** Paul urges us to fill our minds with every good thing.

In spite of what some critics say, Christianity is not a religion of negativity and self-degradation. On the contrary, God's desire for each person—to enjoy life in relationship with him and with others—is as positive as anyone could imagine. Moreover, God's instructions on how to enjoy that life are decidedly positive.

Philippians 4:8, for example, encourages us to focus our minds and our thoughts, not on what's wrong with our lives or ourselves, but on anything excellent or praiseworthy. Specifically, we should meditate on things that are
  ● true: in accordance with the way things really are;
  ● noble: majestic, lofty, and worthy of respect;
  ● right: fair with God, others, and ourselves;
  ● pure: untainted by moral or natural evil;
  ● lovely: eliciting admiration and affection; and
  ● admirable: approved by God and others.

Paul's advice applies to a number of areas, including what we think of ourselves. We should be honest, but fair, with ourselves. In addition, we need to remember the good in our lives and think on the noble, lovely, and admirable aspects of ourselves.

Trying to live with an inaccurate view of who you are makes as much sense as trying to find your way around New York City with a map of Houston. Unfortunately, many people try to find their way around in life using completely incorrect "maps" of their own identities. With wrong beliefs about who they are, they're never quite able to find happiness or themselves.

It's not enough for people to know how their self-identities were formed. They must also learn how to sift through beliefs they have about themselves and filter out those that aren't true. Use this lesson to help people uncover and overcome the lies that find their way into their hearts.

THIS LESSON AT A GLANCE

Section	Minutes	What Participants Will Do	Supplies
OPENING	up to 10	**STICKS AND STONES**—Write hurtful and helpful phrases on newspaper bats and talk about how words can destroy or build up.	Newspapers, masking tape, markers
BIBLE EXPLORATION AND APPLICATION	20 to 30	☐ Option 1: **NOTHING TO FEAR BUT FEAR ITSELF**—Find objects that represent their fears, then learn from 1 Samuel 9:25–10:1, 14-24 and 15:1-26 how false beliefs often lead to failure.	Newsprint, markers, paper, pencils
	15 to 20	☐ Option 2: **THROUGH OTHERS' EYES**—Explore how some situations create false self-images, then learn biblical thruths to combat those false self-images.	"Others' Eyes" handouts (pp. 37-39), pencils, Bibles
CLOSING	up to 5	**COMMITMENT TO TRUTH**—Write thank you cards to God.	Thank you cards, pencils
FOR EXTRA TIME	up to 10	**I'M A CHILD OF GOD**—Discover what Matthew 7:7-11; Romans 8:15-17; Galatians 4:4-6; and James 1:16-18 teach about who they are as children of God.	
	up to 10	**ELDERS' EYES**—Discuss how their self-images have been shaped by significant people from their past.	

Sticks and Stones

(up to 10 minutes)

To begin class, give each person one or two sections of a newspaper and a marker. Have each person create a "newspaper bat" by rolling up the newspaper and taping each end. Instruct everyone to write on one side of the newspaper bat a hurtful word or phrase that was used against him or her at some time in the past. Then instruct class members to write affirming words or phrases on the other sides of their bats.

When everyone is finished, form a circle. Have class members take turns telling what they wrote and explaining the situations in which the words or phrases were used.

After everyone has shared, tell people to perform some action with their bats. Encourage class members to do whatever they want with their bats. For example, people may play baseball, engage in a mock sword fight, pretend to threaten others, or tape several bats together to create a sculpture.

After everyone has done something with his or her bat, re-form the circle and ask:

● **How could we use the newspaper bats in a positive way?** (We could create a sculpture with them; we could start a campfire; we could play a game.)

● **How could we use the newspaper bats in a negative way?** (We could hit someone; we could threaten or intimidate people.)

● **How are words like our newspaper bats? How are they different?** (We can use words to build others up; we can injure others with words; words are more powerful than any newspaper bat.)

Say: **The words you hear about yourself have a powerful impact on your self-concept. This is especially true when you're young and the words come from someone with authority in your life. But not everything people said about you in the past was true.** ▶ **Let's explore how lies we believe about ourselves can influence the way we live our lives.**

TEACHER TIP

If you have more than eight people in your class, form multiple circles of eight or fewer.

THE POINT ▶

BIBLE EXPLORATION AND APPLICATION

☐ OPTION 1:
Nothing to Fear But Fear Itself
(20 to 30 minutes)

Have everyone search the room for objects that represent fears they have about work, home, the future, their relationships, or some other aspect of their personal lives. Tell class members that they can each gather as many items as they want, but each person must gather at least one item.

After everyone has gathered at least one item, have adults explain their items and the fears they represent. On your own paper, keep a list of the fears mentioned so you can discuss them later.

After everyone has shared, say: **Some of our fears are natural and healthy. For example, it's perfectly normal to be afraid when we stand near the edge of a cliff. Fear is an emotion designed to keep us out of dangerous or life-threatening situations. But sometimes fear is unhealthy. Sometimes our fears are based on false beliefs we have about ourselves. Let's examine how fear destroyed Israel's first king, Saul.**

Form groups of four and assign one-half of the groups **1 Samuel 9:25–10:1, 14-24** and the other half of the groups **1 Samuel 15:1-26**. Instruct groups to read their passages then discuss the following questions. To help groups remember the questions, write them on a sheet of newsprint and hang it in a prominent place.

- What fears does Saul appear to have?
- What faulty beliefs might have produced these fears?
- To what extent were Saul's fears justified?
- How did Saul's fears affect his behavior?
- What could Saul have done to overcome his fears?

Allow approximately 10 minutes for discussion, then form new foursomes to include two people who studied each biblical passage. Allow group members several minutes to report their discoveries with one another.

Then say: **It's pretty obvious that Saul was afraid to act like a king because he didn't think of himself as a king. Unfortunately, the same thing happens with people today. For example, someone who's always afraid of losing her job may have a false belief about her own competence. Likewise, someone who's always afraid his wife is cheating on him may have a false belief about his own self-worth.**

Read the list of fears people mentioned at the beginning of this activity, but without indicating who said what. Then

TEACHER TIP

If the room in which you're meeting doesn't contain many items, bring a number of odds and ends of small items for class members to use in this activity. You can also have class members use objects from their pockets, wallets, or purses.

TEACHER TIP

If you have a group larger than eight, consider forming several groups of eight or fewer.

TEACHER TIP

To form the new foursomes quickly, instruct members of the original foursomes to choose partners, then have each pair join a pair that studied the other biblical passage.

This may be a good time to remind people of the commitment they made last week to protect one another's dignity and to keep the conversations held in this class private. This may help some people feel more comfortable in opening up.

THE POINT ▷

instruct groups to discuss the following questions. Ask volunteers to report their groups' insights after each question. Ask:

● **How are the fears we discussed earlier like Saul's fears? How are they different?** (Like Saul, we're afraid that people won't like us; we're also afraid of failure; unlike Saul, we don't have to worry about public humiliation.)

● **What beliefs do these fears point to?** (We believe that our worth depends on what people think of us; we believe that we're going to disappoint God.)

● **To what extent are these beliefs false? To what extent are they true?** (Our worth depends on what God thinks, not what people think; God doesn't expect us to do things we're not equipped to do.)

Give each person a sheet of paper and a pencil. Direct class members to create three columns on their papers. Then have them list in the columns: (1) the fears their objects represent, (2) any false beliefs those fears might be connected to, and (3) what steps they can take to change those false beliefs. For example, someone might write: (1) I'm afraid no one likes me. (2) My value is based on what I do, not who I am. (3) Memorize verses about God's unconditional love for me.

When everyone is done writing, say: ▷ **The lies we believe about ourselves can control our lives. But half the battle in overcoming false beliefs about ourselves is simply recognizing what the lies are. Take your paper home and use it as a reminder to battle the lies you believe about yourself with the truth of who you are as a special child of God.**

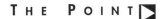

FOR *Even Deeper*
DISCUSSION

● How well did God equip Saul to serve as king? Does God ever ask us to do things he hasn't prepared us to do? Explain.

● Read 1 John 4:18a. Is it wrong to be afraid? Why or why not? When might fear be a good thing? How can God's love turn our fears into something positive?

If you have more than 18 class members, form groups of six and assign the same situation to multiple groups.

☐ **OPTION 2:**
Through Others' Eyes
(15 to 20 minutes)

Before class, photocopy the "Others' Eyes" handout (pp. 37-39). Make three copies or, if you have more than 18 in your class, one copy for every six people.

Form three groups and give each group pencils and a copy of the "Others' Eyes" handout. Assign a different situation to each group. Have each group follow the instructions on the handout.

When groups are finished, have them report back what they discovered. Then have groups discuss the following questions. Ask:

● **How are the situations on the handout similar to situations in your life?** Answers will vary.

● **How much is your self-identity influenced by others?** (I think I'm strongly affected by how my father views me; it's hard to feel good about myself when others make me feel unimportant.)

● **How can you discover whether or not something you believe about yourself is true?** (I can ask friends to help me see the truth; I can pray to God for peace; I can evaluate what I feel on the basis of what I know.)

Read **Philippians 4:8.** Ask:

● **What truths about yourself should you focus on?** (God knows me better than anyone else does, and he loves me for who I am; my worth isn't based on what I do.)

Say: ▶ **Lies we believe about ourselves can influence and even control the way we live. That's why it's important to concentrate on the true, noble, lovely, and admirable things about ourselves. We can overcome the negative influence of inaccurate self-images by comparing our self-beliefs with what the Bible and our Christian brothers and sisters say is true about us.**

■■■■■■■■■■■■■■■■■■■■■■■■■■■

 For *Even Deeper* DISCUSSION

● John 8:44 teaches that Satan is the father of lies. Why does Satan want us to believe lies about ourselves? How does Satan get us to believe those lies? What can we do to combat those lies?

● To what extent should we think about negative things in our lives such as sin, loss, and failure? How can these things be part of focusing on what is excellent and praiseworthy?

■■■■■■■■■■■■■■■■■■■■■■■■■■■

APPLY•IT•TO **LIFE** THIS WEEK   The "Apply-It-To-Life This Week" handout (p. 40) helps people further explore the issues uncovered in today's class. Give everyone a photocopy of the handout. Encourage class members to take time during the coming week to explore the questions and activities listed on the handout.

This may be an emotional activity for some as they think about abusive or difficult childhoods. Encourage group members to support each other in this activity by allowing someone to cry or to pass if he or she is simply too uncomfortable to talk about the past.

◀ T H E   P O I N T

 **BIBLE** INSIGHT

The Greek word translated "think about" in Philippians 4:8 is *logizomai.* It means both "to evaluate critically" and "to ponder in one's mind." Paul seems to have both meanings in mind here. Paul wants us to evaluate everything (including what we believe about ourselves) to identify what is true, noble, and so forth. But then we're to focus and carefully reflect upon these true or noble things so they influence and shape our actions.

Commitment to Truth

(up to 5 minutes)

Form a circle and distribute blank thank you cards and pencils. Read **Philippians 4:8.**

Say: **As God's children, we need to fill our minds with things that are true, noble, right, pure, lovely, and admirable. That includes the things we think about ourselves. Take a moment and silently ask God to show you one thing about yourself that is true** (pause), **one thing that is noble** (pause), **one thing that is right** (pause), **one thing that is pure** (pause), **one thing that is lovely** (pause), **and one thing that is admirable** (pause). **Now write a thank you prayer to God for each of these things and ask God to help you to continue seeking the truth about yourself until you fully discover who you are in Christ.**

Encourage class members to keep the cards in their Bibles and to refer to them often as they seek to uncover their true identities in Christ.

 For Extra Time

I'M A CHILD OF GOD

(up to 10 minutes)

Form small groups. Assign each group one of the following passages: Matthew 7:7-11; Romans 8:15-17; Galatians 4:4-6; James 1:16-18. Have groups discuss what these passages teach about who we are as God's children. Write the references on newsprint and record each group's insights for everyone to see.

ELDERS' EYES

(up to 10 minutes)

Form groups of three or four. Instruct group members to tell about significant people who have helped shape how they see themselves today. As group members share, have them answer these questions:

• **How do you think this person would describe you to a stranger?**

• **What messages did this person give you about yourself?**

• **What's something you wish you could change about the relationship you had with this person?**

■ Others' Eyes—Situation 1

1. **Read the situation below.**

   While Mark was growing up, his father was mayor of the town where his family lived. Even when he was just 6 years old, he knew that his father expected him to be an example of good behavior whenever they were in public. When the family was together at home, which wasn't often, Mark's father spent most of his time in his private study. Mark's mother told Mark that his father really loved him but that his work was very important.

2. **Answer the following questions.**
   ● What false beliefs about himself is Mark likely to have?

   ● What truths about himself may Mark miss because of his experiences?

   ● How might these false beliefs impact Mark's self-identity as an adult?

3. **Read Ephesians 3:17b-19; 1 Peter 2:9; and 1 John 3:1.**

4. **Discuss the following questions.**
   ● How might the truths found in these passages expose the lies Mark believes about himself?

   ● What will Mark need to do to take on the identity God intended for him?

■ Others' Eyes—Situation 2

1. **Read the situation below.**

Carol is a 30-year-old insurance broker. She's married and has two children in school. She's been with the same insurance company for three years and has always received excellent evaluations from her supervisor. Last month she applied for a management position, but the promotion went to Paul, an energetic salesman who joined the company five months ago. The head of personnel told Carol that she and Paul were equally qualified but that Paul was better able to devote himself fully to the position. Carol sometimes had to stay home with a sick child, and occasionally she seemed tired at work.

2. **Answer the following questions.**
- What false beliefs about herself is Carol likely to have?

- What truths about herself may Carol miss because of her situation?

- How might these false beliefs impact Carol's self-identity?

3. **Read 1 Samuel 16:7 and Galatians 3:26-29; 6:9-10.**

4. **Discuss the following questions.**
- How might the truths found in these passages expose the lies Carol believes about herself?

- What will Carol need to do to take on the identity God intended for her?

◼ Others' Eyes—Situation 3

1. **Read the situation below.**

   Three years ago, after 15 years of marriage, Stephen's wife left him. The couple rarely fought, but the marriage was cold and unfulfilling for both. Since then Stephen has done his best to care for his three children, who live with him during the school year. He tries to balance work demands with household responsibilities such as cooking, cleaning, and laundry, but the kids either complain that he spends too much time at work or that he doesn't do a very good job taking care of them. Last month, Stephen's ex-wife announced that she is remarrying and would like the kids to live with her and her new husband. Stephen left the decision up to his kids, and they decided to move in with their mom as soon as school ends.

2. **Answer the following questions.**
   - What false beliefs about himself is Stephen likely to have?

   - What truths about himself may Stephen miss because of his situation?

   - How might these false beliefs affect Stephen's self-identity?

3. **Read Deuteronomy 31:6; John 16:33; and Philippians 4:19.**

4. **Discuss the following questions.**
   - How might the truths found in these passages expose the lies Stephen believes about himself?

   - What will Stephen need to do to take on the identity God intended for him?

Living the Lies

The Point: ▶ Lies we believe about ourselves can influence the way we live our lives.

Scripture Focus: 1 Samuel 9:25–10:1, 14-24; 15:1-26; and Philippians 4:8

Reflecting on God's Word

Each day this week, read one of the following Scriptures and examine if what it says is true of you. Then examine how well you are acting upon that truth in your life. You may want to list your discoveries in the space under each passage.

Day 1: Romans 8:31-39. Nothing can separate us from God's love.

Day 2: 1 Corinthians 6:19-20. Our bodies are temples of the Holy Spirit.

Day 3: Galatians 5:1. Christ set us free and wants us to live as free people.

Day 4: Ephesians 1:3-10. In Christ, God has blessed us with every spiritual blessing.

Day 5: Colossians 1:9-14. God has rescued us from darkness and placed us in Christ's kingdom.

Day 6: 2 Peter 1:3-9. God has given us everything we need to please him.

Beyond Reflection

1. List the people who have been most influential in shaping your self-identity. Beside each person's name, write in detail how that person influenced you and what he or she taught you about yourself (either good or bad). If possible, call or write some of the people on the list to ask what their impressions of you really are. Ask God to help you uncover any false beliefs about yourself that may have sprung from those relationships.

2. Consider reading a book that explores the lies we believe about ourselves and the process of replacing those lies with the truth. Some suggestions include *The Search for Significance* by Robert S. McGee; *Telling Yourself the Truth* by William Backus and Marie Chapian; and *His Imprint, My Expression* by Kay Arthur.

Next Week's Bible Passages: Romans 8:31-39 and Ephesians 2:1-10

Who Am I, Really?

Our true identities are found only in Christ.

◀ T H E   P O I N T

OBJECTIVES

Participants will
- examine what the Bible says about who they are in Christ,
- discuss how their identities in Christ should affect the way they view themselves, and
- counteract negative feelings about themselves with the truth of who they are in Christ.

BIBLE BASIS

Look up the Scriptures. Then read the following background sections to see how the passages relate to people today.

In **Romans 8:31-39,** Paul tells us that nothing can separate us from God's love.

ROMANS 8:31-39

Christians are not exempt from sin and suffering. As residents of a sin-cursed world, we encounter and experience evil in a variety of forms. But we do have an advantage over people who don't know or love Christ. God has promised us that he will turn everything evil in our lives into something good (Romans 8:28-30).

It's against the background of God's promise to turn evil into good that Paul reminds us of our security in Christ. Since God is for us, no one can successfully oppose us. To prove his point, Paul offers several examples of how God is for us.

In the first place, God has already given us the great gift of his Son, so it's unthinkable that he would withhold any other lesser gift. In addition, no one can rightly condemn us. God has forgiven our past sins, and now Jesus represents us before God every day. Even our present sufferings don't disprove God's goodness to us. God's people have always faced opposition, as Paul's quotation of Psalm 44:22 shows (see Romans 8:36). But through God and his love, apparent losses are turned into total victories.

Since nothing can separate us from God's love in Christ, we are free to discover and develop our true identities. Since God is on our side, we can move past guilt and self-condemnation to growth and self-acceptance. In Christ, we find our true identities as those loved by God.

EPHESIANS 2:1-10

In **Ephesians 2:1-10,** Paul explains that God has made us alive in Christ.

Sometimes thinking about who we *were* helps us see who we *are* more clearly. That's the approach Paul takes in the first three verses of this passage. He reminds us that we were once spiritually dead. Enslaved to sin and ruled by Satan, we went wherever and did whatever our hearts desired. Like everyone else without Christ, we lived under God's wrath.

However, that was before Christ. Now we have the basis for entirely new identities in Christ. First, we know that God loves us. God loved us even when we were ruled by sin and death. He loved us, not because of anything we did, but because we are valuable to him. Knowing this should promote a healthy view of our own worth.

God has also made us alive with Christ. God didn't leave Jesus in the grave, and he didn't leave us dead in our sins. With our new life in Christ, we can experience the abundant life that God wants every person to enjoy (John 10:10). We don't have to serve sin or fear death, for we are free to truly live.

In addition, we reign in heaven with Christ. When God raised Christ to heaven, he took us with him. We still live on this earth, to be sure, but our life is in heaven with Christ. We're no longer under Satan's dominion. In fact, since we are in heaven with Christ, we are above this world and Satan, its ruler.

Finally, God has enabled us to do good. While our feeling of self-worth derives from God's love for us, our sense of purpose stems from the task God has given us. God wants us to perform good deeds that honor him. Our lives aren't pointless or of little consequence. Because of who we are in Christ, we can make a difference in the world and in the lives of others.

It's important to learn how inaccurate self-images affect the way we think, act, and relate to others, but it's not enough. We also need to see ourselves as God sees us. We need to understand who we are in Christ. Use this lesson to help the people in your class shape their views of themselves according to their true identities in Christ.

THIS LESSON AT A GLANCE

Section	Minutes	What Participants Will Do	Supplies
OPENING	up to 10	**SECRET IDENTITIES**—Discuss which make-believe characters they most identify with.	
BIBLE EXPLORATION AND APPLICATION	20 to 30	□ Option 1: **DESIGNED FOR LIVING**—Create floor plans for their own dream houses and learn God's design for them from Ephesians 2:1-10.	Bibles, newsprint, pencils, marker
	20 to 25	□ Option 2: **WHO GOD SAYS I AM**—Discover how the truths of Romans 8:31-39 and Ephesians 2:1-10 can change negative feelings they have about themselves.	Bibles, "I Say/God Says" handout (p. 50), pencils
CLOSING	up to 10	**GOD'S NAMES FOR ME**—Think up positive names for each other.	3×5 cards, pencils
FOR EXTRA TIME	up to 10	**PERSONAL PROFILES**—Start writing profiles of who they really are.	Paper, pencils
	up to 10	**FAITH BUILDER**—Pray with partners about lies they believe about themselves and truths about themselves they have a hard time believing.	

Secret Identities
(up to 10 minutes)

Begin class by forming groups of six. Instruct class members to discuss the following question in their groups. Ask:

● **If you could be any character in a movie, TV show, or novel, who would you be? Why?**

After everyone has answered, ask for volunteers to share their groups' responses by answering the following questions. Ask:

● **What kinds of characters did your group members choose?** (Characters with qualities they admire; characters who have gone through similar experiences; characters who live exciting lives.)

● **Why do you think we identify with these kinds of characters?** (We're not satisfied with our own lives; we like to feel that there are other people like us; we want to be the best we can be.)

Say: **It's often tempting to try to find our identities in others. Generally we don't lose ourselves in make-believe characters, but sometimes we try to find ourselves in a spouse, a child, someone we admire, or a close friend. Unfortunately, we'll never find ourselves completely in these people. Today we're going to talk about how ▷ our true identities are found only in Christ.**

THE POINT ▷

Lead the class in prayer, asking God to help class members understand and sense the depth of Christ's love for them. Then encourage class members to get involved in the discussions and activities during the study.

TEACHER TIP

You may want to set up tables for this activity so participants will have an easier time drawing their floor plans. In addition, if you don't have access to newsprint, regular-sized paper will work well. If you prefer not to have class members sketch their floor plans, form groups of four and have group members describe their dream houses to one another.

☐ **OPTION 1:**

Designed for Living
(20 to 30 minutes)

Give each person a sheet of newsprint and a pencil. Tell class members to draw floor plans of their dream homes on the newsprint. Encourage them to use their imaginations and include in their floor plans anything that would make them happy, no matter how unusual it may seem.

When everyone has completed a floor plan, form groups of four. Direct group members to describe their dream homes to each other. Then have class members discuss the following questions in their groups. Ask volunteers to share insights from their discussions with the rest of the class. Ask:

● **How do you feel about your dream home ideas?** (I'm excited about it; I wish it really existed so I could live in it; I can't wait to show it to my husband.)

● **What does the design of your dream home reveal about who you are?** (I like being a dad, so I have lots of space for kids; I grew up poor, so my house is smaller than some people's; I'm a loner, so my house provides a lot of privacy.)

● **How is your design of a dream house like God's design of you?** (Both reflect the true nature of their designers; there's a reason for everything in both designs.)

Say: **The way we design our homes tells a lot about the way we live. In the same way, we can learn a great deal about who we really are by examining how God has designed us.**

Direct class members to read **Ephesians 2:1-10.** While they are reading, write the following questions on newsprint and hang it in a prominent place. Tell groups to answer the questions on the basis of **Ephesians 2:1-10** and to be prepared to share their answers with the rest of the class after 10 minutes.

● What are the characteristics of those without Christ?

● What are the characteristics of those in Christ?

● What is God's attitude toward us?

● How should who we are in Christ affect the way we live?

After 10 minutes, ask for volunteers to share their groups' insights with the rest of the class. Then say: **Because of God's love for us in Christ, we are no longer bound by the sins and pains of the past. We are free to experience and enjoy the life that God designed for each of us. Let's take a few minutes to talk about that design and how it should affect our views of ourselves.**

Instruct class members to discuss the following questions in their groups. Ask:

● **How does it make you feel to know how much God loves you?** (Secure; completely accepted; safe; valuable.)

● **How should this influence the way we view ourselves?** (Since God accepts us, we can accept ourselves; we shouldn't base our self-worth on what we do; we're free to be who we really are.)

● **How does it make you feel to realize that God has made you alive?** (Hopeful; empowered; free.)

Ephesians 2:8-9 teaches that salvation is based on God's grace and secured through our faith. Salvation is a product of grace, not of our own efforts or works. Salvation becomes ours when we place our trust in Christ, but it is entirely God's gift to us. A proper self-identity begins when we understand that all we are is based on who God has made us to be.

● **How should this influence the way we view ourselves?** (We can put past sins and pains behind us; we have the power to enjoy life to its fullest; we're no longer slaves to sin and death.)

● **How does it make you feel to recognize that you are Christ's representative on earth?** (Nervous; honored; trusted.)

● **How should this influence the way we view ourselves?** (We're agents of God's love; we have a reason to be here; God believes in us, so we can believe in ourselves.)

Say: **Since God designed us, he knows us better than anyone else, including ourselves. Now take a moment to ask God what his design for you is. Silently answer the following questions and ask God's Spirit to help you see yourself as God designed you.** Ask:

● **What special abilities or gifts has God given you?** Pause.

● **What character strengths has God given you?** Pause.

● **What experiences has God used to help you grow?** Pause.

● **What does God like the most about you?** Pause.

● **What area would God like to see the most improvement in?** Pause.

Say: **God loves us unconditionally, wants us to live contentedly, and trusts us completely to represent him. Since ▷ our true identities are found only in Christ, we need to set aside all of the inaccurate blueprints we have of ourselves and build our lives according to God's perfect design.**

T H E   P O I N T ▷

■■■■■■■■■■■■■■■■■■■■■■■■■■■■

FOR *Even Deeper*
DISCUSSION

● Paul states that God has already "seated us with [Christ] in the heavenly realms" (Ephesians 2:6b, New International Version). What does this mean?

● How should the teaching of Ephesians 2:6 affect how we view ourselves? how we view our place in this world?

■■■■■■■■■■■■■■■■■■■■■■■■■■■■

☐ **O P T I O N   2 :**

*Who God
Says I Am*

(20 to 25 minutes)

Before class, make one copy of the "I Say/God Says" handout (p. 50) for each person in your class.

Form groups of four (or keep the foursomes from the "Designed for

Living" activity). Say: **It's easy to say that ▶ our true identities are found only in Christ, but sometimes it's difficult to know how that should shape what we think of ourselves. We all have negative feelings about ourselves, and those feelings can choke out the love and acceptance available in Christ.**

Give each person a pencil and a copy of the "I Say/God Says" handout. Instruct everyone to take several minutes to complete the "I Say" section of the handout.

After several minutes, say: **If we understand who we are in Christ, each one of the negative feelings we listed can be changed into something positive. Work together in your groups to complete the "God Says" section of the handout. In 15 minutes, we'll report back on what we discovered.**

After 15 minutes, ask for volunteers to share their groups' insights with the rest of the class. Then have groups discuss the following questions. Ask:

● **How hard was it for you to talk about negative feelings you have about yourself?** (It was hard to admit that I'm not as confident as people think I am; it was difficult at first, but writing down my negative feelings helped me see how unfounded they are.)

● **How is that like the difficulty of overcoming those feelings?** (Sometimes it's easier to ignore my problems than to solve them; it gets easier if we keep at it.)

● **What makes it difficult to think or talk about these feelings?** (We're afraid that we're the only ones who have them; we feel there's nothing we can do about them; we don't want to relive old pains.)

Then have everyone silently answer the following questions. Ask:

● **What negative feeling do you struggle with the most?** Pause.

● **What is the source or cause of this negative feeling?** Pause.

● **How can your identity in Christ change this negative feeling?** Pause.

● **In what specific ways can you remind yourself of who you are in Christ?** Pause.

Say: **Now take a few moments to pray together with your group members for God to plant each of the truths you've discovered deep in your heart. After you pray, tell each group member one positive thing about ▶ his or her true identity, as found in Christ. For example, you might say, "Frank, since God is for you, there's no problem you can't solve."**

For *Even Deeper*
DISCUSSION

● Romans 8:31-39 teaches that no natural or supernatural force can separate us from God's love. Can we sever ourselves from God's love? To what extent can we frustrate God's good will for our lives?

● Are guilt or shame always negative? If not, how can we tell the difference between proper and improper feelings of guilt? How can we transform those negative feelings into something good?

APPLY■IT■TO **LIFE** THIS WEEK   The "Apply-It-To-Life This Week" handout (p. 51) helps people further explore the issues uncovered in today's class. Give everyone a photocopy of the handout. Encourage class members to take time during the coming week to explore the questions and activities listed on the handout.

CLOSING

God's Names for Me
(up to 10 minutes)

Keep class members in their groups of four. Give each person a 3×5 card and a pencil.

THE POINT ▷

Say: **One by one, pray for each person in your group, asking God to raise up that person's** ▷ **true identity in Christ in his or her heart. After you pray for each people, write descriptive "names" that fit those person's true identity on his or her card. For example, I see several people who could be named "compassion" or "mercy." Choose names that fit those people's special identities in Christ.**

Dismiss groups after they finish praying. Encourage everyone to keep the "name tag" as a reminder of his or her true identity in Christ.

For Extra Time

PERSONAL PROFILES
(up to 10 minutes)

Give everyone a sheet of paper and a pencil. Have each class member write a rough draft of a personal profile based on what he or she has learned so far in the course. For example, people may want to begin listing their strengths, weaknesses, interests, goals, priorities, and so on. Encourage adults to work on their statements even after the course is over. Tell them to refer to their personal profiles often, especially when they need to make important decisions in their lives.

FAITH BUILDER
(up to 10 minutes)

Have class members choose prayer partners. Once they've paired up, have each partner complete the following sentences:
- One lie about me that I find easy to believe is...
- One truth about me that I find hard to believe is...

Once partners have shared, have them pray together, asking God to help them stop believing lies about themselves and start living according to the truth of who they are in Christ.

■ I Say/God Says

I SAY

Complete the "I Say" section of this handout on your own. Be as honest as you can. You won't have to share any information that you don't want to share.

1. Think about negative feelings you sometimes have about yourself.

2. In the space below, write words or phrases that describe those negative feelings. For example, you might write "inadequate" or "not well-liked."

GOD SAYS

Complete the "God Says" section of your handout with your group members. You have 15 minutes to complete this section.

1. Read Romans 8:31-39. List what this passage teaches about who you are in Christ and how God feels about you.

2. Read Ephesians 2:1-10. List what this passage teaches about who you are in Christ and how God feels about you.

3. To the extent that you feel comfortable, discuss with your group members how the biblical truths you listed above refute, counterbalance, or enable you to change the negative feelings you listed in the "I Say" section.

4. Record any insights opposite the negative feelings you wrote in the "I Say" section.

Who Am I, Really?

The Point: ▶ Our true identities are found only in Christ.

Scripture Focus: Romans 8:31-39 and Ephesians 2:1-10

Reflecting on God's Word

Each day this week, read one of the following Scriptures and examine what it says about your identity in Christ. Then examine how well you're reflecting that part of your identity in your daily life. You may want to list your discoveries in the space under each passage.

Day 1: John 14:15-21. Jesus loves us and will never leave us.

Day 2: John 15:9-17. We are Christ's friends and loved ones.

Day 3: 1 Peter 2:9-12. We are the people of God.

Day 4: 1 Corinthians 1:26-31. God uses our weaknesses to show his strength.

Day 5: Romans 6:1-14. We have been freed from sin's power.

Day 6: Ephesians 5:8-21. We are children of the light.

Beyond Reflection

1. Go on a "positive trait" search. Contact people from your past, such as parents, old friends, teachers or other important persons, and ask these people to tell you the things they like(d) best about you. Keep a record of all the things people say, then pray about the list, asking the Holy Spirit to help you sift through what people have said to find a true image of who God created you to be.

2. Based on the things you've discovered about yourself, choose one new activity, hobby, or sport that reflects your true identity and start learning about it this week. Set a goal to make that new activity a regular part of your life within the next six months.

Next Week's Bible Passages: Philippians 3:7-14 and 2 Timothy 4:6-8

From Here to Eternity

With God's help, we can live fulfilled, purposeful lives.

◄ **T H E   P O I N T**

OBJECTIVES

Participants will
- discuss the different roles they fill in life,
- identify what they want to be remembered for, and
- begin to write personal mission statements.

BIBLE BASIS

Look up the Scriptures. Then read the following background sections to see how the passages relate to people today.

In **Philippians 3:7-14,** Paul describes the guiding purpose of his life.

PHILIPPIANS 3:7-14

Before his conversion, Paul sought fulfillment and acceptance by scrupulously keeping every detail of the Law (Philippians 3:4b-6). However, that changed when Christ met him on the road to Damascus (Acts 9:1-19). When Paul understood what Christ wanted from him, Paul surrendered his own agenda and gave himself fully to Christ.

Paul's new relationship with Jesus brought a total change in values. Earlier Paul had sought to become righteous before God by keeping the Law. Now he recognized that all that was rubbish. There was only one way to become righteous. Paul had to trust Jesus to make him acceptable to God. Since everything depended on Jesus, all that really mattered was knowing him.

As soon as he trusted Jesus, Paul's life had a new purpose. He wanted to know Jesus as fully and as intimately as he could. Paul wanted to identify with Jesus in every possible way. He sought to experience the good—the power God demonstrated when he raised Jesus from the dead. But Paul also was willing to go through the bad, even to the extent of sharing in Jesus' sufferings and death. Paul so valued his relationship with Jesus that he devoted his life to knowing and identifying with him.

However, Paul's surrender of himself to Christ was not an act of passive resignation. On the contrary, Paul strained and struggled to fulfill Christ's goal for his life. Like a runner pressing on toward the finish line, Paul pressed on to receive the prize for which Christ had called him. Paul was neither constrained nor controlled by his past. All that mattered was his present preoccupation with knowing Christ a little better each day.

Paul's life was not purposeless before he trusted Jesus, but it was unfulfilled. Though Paul devoted himself to obeying the Law, he never found the peace and acceptance that he craved. As soon as Paul devoted himself to Jesus, his life was both purposeful and satisfying. Like Paul, people today need to realize that the only basis for a fulfilled, purposeful life is a vital, intimate relationship with Jesus.

2 TIMOTHY 4:6-8

In **2 Timothy 4:6-8,** Paul reflects on his life of service to Christ.

Paul's life was nearly over when he wrote 2 Timothy. From a human perspective, things couldn't have been worse. Paul was alone in a cold Roman prison, certain he would be sentenced to death any day (2 Timothy 1:16-17; 4:9-18). But Paul wasn't worried. He was ready to die. Paul had lived a faithful and meaningful life, so he could face death calmly and confidently, without fear or regret.

Paul's confidence even caused him to look positively toward his execution. Paul had given his life to Jesus. Now his death would complete the sacrifice. Just as the ancient Israelites poured wine over their sacrifices to create aromas pleasing to God, Paul was pouring out his life and blood as the ultimate sacrifice to God (see Numbers 15:1-10). Moreover, death wasn't the end; it was a departure. In death, Paul was being "loosed" (Greek, *analusis*) in the same way that a ship setting sail is loosed from its moorings.

Paul's courage in the face of death arose from the confidence of a life well-lived. Like a runner who had successfully finished a race, Paul looked back on his life with pride and satisfaction. He had kept the faith. He had protected all that Christ had entrusted to him. So just as an athlete of his day received a laurel wreath for winning a race, Paul would receive a crown when his race was over.

Everyone wants to feel as though his or her life has purpose. But sometimes it's difficult to know how or where to find it. Like Paul, we search for meaning in self-improvement or good deeds, but neither of these brings lasting fulfillment. We need to learn, as Paul did, that the only purposeful *and* fulfilling life is the life given fully to knowing Jesus. We need to understand that only as we devote ourselves to Christ can we discover and develop our true potentials.

THIS LESSON AT A GLANCE

Section	Minutes	What Participants Will Do	Supplies
OPENING	*up to 10*	**ROLE PLAYING**—Cover themselves with labels that reflect their roles in everyday life.	Self-adhesive, blank name tags; newsprint; tape; markers
BIBLE EXPLORATION AND APPLICATION	*20 to 30*	☐ *Option 1:* **MY EULOGY**—Write their own eulogies.	Paper, pencils, Bibles, newsprint, markers
	15 to 20	☐ *Option 2:* **FROM HERE TO ETERNITY**—Create rough drafts of their personal mission statements.	Paper, pencils, newsprint, markers
CLOSING	*up to 10*	**PURPOSEFUL ADDITIONS**—Write additions to each other's eulogies or purpose statements.	Pencils
FOR EXTRA TIME	*up to 10*	**CIRCLE BLESSING**—Affirm each other by identifying areas of growth or potential.	
	up to 10	**NEW DIRECTIONS**—Review what they've learned and discuss how they can apply it in their lives.	

Role Playing

(up to 10 minutes)

As you begin the class, tell adults what they'll be learning and doing in today's lesson. Use the following statement or your own summary of the main point: **Welcome to our last class on seeing ourselves as God sees us. We've already learned how our identities are formed, how we can recognize false beliefs about ourselves, and how our true identities are found only in Christ. Today we're going to discuss how to live ▶ the fulfilled, purposeful lives that God wants us to live.**

Tape a sheet of newsprint to the wall and ask class members to brainstorm all the roles that people fill in everyday life. For example, they might list "father," "sister," "leader," "friend," "employee," "neighbor," "consumer," and so forth. When you have an extensive list, give each person a stack of name tags and a marker.

Say: **Write each of the roles you fill on a separate name tag. Draw a star on roles that you think especially fit your identity, such as "adventurer" or "student." Once you have a fairly complete list, stick the name tags to your clothing so others can read them.**

When everyone is ready, direct class members to mingle and read each other's roles. After several minutes, ask them to return to their seats.

Say: **Now put any roles you don't enjoy on your left side and any roles you do enjoy on your right side.**

After everyone has done this, form groups of four or fewer to discuss the following questions. Instruct everyone to form groups with people who have roles significantly different from theirs. Ask:

● **Which roles fit your true identity the best? Explain.** (Since I'm friendly, I make a good neighbor; God has given me a good mind, so I like being a student.)

● **Which roles don't fit your true identity very well? Explain.** (I hate working in an office environment, because I'd rather be outside; I don't like being a housewife—I'd much rather have an outside career of my own.)

● **What can you do to better match your roles to who you are?** (I can look for a different job; I can stop trying to be involved in so many different things at church; I can join a health club to become more physically fit.)

Say: **We can avoid feeling that life is just carrying us along by setting personal goals for the roles we fill in life. Today we're going to start that process. It'll be the first step ▶ to living the fulfilled, purposeful lives that God wants us to enjoy.**

T H E   P O I N T ▶

T E A C H E R

If you are unable to gather enough name tags, give everyone a sheet of paper and a pencil. Instruct everyone to list the roles he or she fills on the paper. Have people list roles they don't enjoy on the left side of the paper and those they do enjoy on the right side.

T H E   P O I N T ▶

☐ **OPTION 1:**
My Eulogy
(20 to 30 minutes)

Say: **To help us clarify what kind of people we really want to be, let's try something a little unusual. Let's write our own eulogies. However, instead of writing what someone might say about you now, write what you would like to be remembered for at the end of your life.**

Give everyone a sheet of paper and a pencil. As class members write their ideal eulogies, encourage them to think in terms of what would happen if they lived the rest of their lives in the best way possible, not in terms of the lives they've already lived.

When everyone is finished, have each person tell what he or she wrote. If you have more than 10 in your class, form two or three groups for the sharing time and the discussion questions.

After everyone has shared, ask:

● **How is your ideal eulogy different from the eulogy someone would write about you today? How is it the same?** (My ideal eulogy focuses more on family accomplishments; both eulogies talk a lot about my career.)

● **What did you learn from writing your own ideal eulogy?** (It made me question my priorities in life today; it convinced me that I need to be more focused; it showed me how much energy I spend on unimportant things.)

Say: **In our culture, people often have career goals, physical fitness goals, or even marriage goals. But it's rare to find a person who has a clear set of "character" goals. Few people think seriously about questions such as "What kind of person do I want to become?" or "What do I really want to be remembered for?" However, Paul was such a person.**

Form groups of four and have each group read **Philippians 3:7-14.** While groups are reading, write these questions on newsprint and hang it in a prominent place.

● What were Paul's goals in terms of accomplishments?

● What were Paul's goals in terms of character development?

● What motivated Paul to pursue these goals?

Give groups five minutes to discuss the questions, then ask for volunteers to share their groups' conclusions with the rest of the class. Then have groups read **2 Timothy 4:6-8.** While groups are reading, write these questions on the sheet of newsprint.

● How well did Paul accomplish what he set out to do?

● To what extent did Paul become the person he wanted to be?

● What do you think enabled Paul to accomplish his goals?

Give groups five minutes to discuss the questions, then ask for volunteers to report their groups' insights with the rest of the class. After every group has shared, have each person write the answers to the following questions on his or her eulogy paper. Pause at least a minute after each question. Ask:

● **What things would you like to accomplish in your life?** Pause.

● **What obstacles or challenges stand in your way?** Pause.

● **What steps can you take to overcome these obstacles?** Pause.

● **What personal qualities do you want to develop?** Pause.

● **What do you need to do to develop these qualities?** Pause.

T H E   P O I N T ▷

When everyone is finished, have each person share one goal-related prayer request with his or her group members. Have groups pray for each of its members' requests. After groups are finished praying, say: ▷ **With God's help, we can live fulfilled, purposeful lives. But it won't just happen. We need to plan to reach the full potential of our true identities in Christ.**

■ ■

FOR *Even Deeper*
DISCUSSION

● Søren Kierkegaard wrote, "Purity of heart is to will one thing." If money, time, and energy were no object, what one thing would you will to do with your life?

● In Philippians 3:12, Paul implies that, although he is not yet perfect, someday he will be. How perfect can we become in this life? How do we grow toward perfection? What would a perfect version of you be like?

■ ■

☐ OPTION 2:
From Here to Eternity
(15 to 20 minutes)

Say: **A useful way to begin setting personal goals is to write a personal mission statement. Personal mission statements describe who we want to be and what we want to do. They also list the values and priorities that are important to us. Personal mission statements are useful tools for giving direction to our lives and for helping with decisions and choices we have to make.**

Give each person two sheets of paper and a pencil. Form groups of four. (If you completed Option 1, form new foursomes.) Instruct groups to read **Philippians 3:7-14.** While groups are reading, write the following phrases on newsprint and hang it in a prominent place.

- gifts or abilities God has given me
- personal characteristics I want to develop
- kinds of relationships I want
- my primary mission in life
- how God wants me to use my gifts or abilities
- my priorities in life
- what I want to accomplish with my life

Say: **To gain some experience composing a personal mission statement, work with your group members and write a personal mission statement as though you were Paul. Use Philippians 3:7-14 as your main source of information about Paul. As much as possible, provide answers for each of the categories on the newsprint. After five minutes, we'll compare the statements.**

After five minutes, have a representative from each group report the main points of his or her group's personal mission statement for Paul. Then ask:

- **What impresses you the most about Paul's personal mission statement?** (Paul is willing to give up everything for Christ; Paul's devotion to Christ puts the rest of his life in focus; Paul's view of himself is honest.)

- **Which values or priorities do you share with Paul?** (Christ comes first in my life, too; like Paul, I want a deeper relationship with Christ.)

- **Which of Paul's goals do you want to make your own?** (I want to experience the power of Jesus' resurrection; I want to live my life to the fullest to the very end.)

Say: **In the next five minutes, I want you to begin to write your own personal mission statement. As before, refer to the categories on the newsprint to help you get started.**

After five minutes, have group members share with each other what they've written. Encourage group mem-

TEACHER TIP

To learn more about personal mission statements, consult Stephen R. Covey's *The Seven Habits of Highly Effective People.*

BIBLE INSIGHT

The knowledge Paul speaks of in Philippians 3:8 (noun: *gnōsis*) and 10 (verb: *ginōskō*) is more than intellectual understanding. The Greek root Paul uses refers to knowledge gained through experience, as opposed to knowledge gained through reflection. When it's applied to knowledge of another person, it refers to knowing someone personally, not merely knowing about someone. Paul isn't content to know more facts about Jesus. He wants a deeper personal relationship with him.

TEACHER
TIP

If people find it hard to get started on their personal mission statements, encourage them to choose elements of Paul's statement to include in their own. Also, make sure people understand that their purpose statements are designed to help *them*, not anyone else. They can be written in any form or with any words they choose, whatever works best for each individual.

bers to point out strengths of each other's statements.

After everyone has shared, say: ▷ **With God's help, we can live fulfilled, purposeful lives. Creating a personal mission statement is an important way to begin living the life we have in Christ. But a personal mission statement can't be finished in five minutes. Continue working on your statement until you're satisfied with what it says. Your statement will probably change as you grow as a person and as a Christian. As you learn more about who you are in Christ, revise your statement to reflect your true identity in him.**

■ ■

 FOR *Even Deeper*
DISCUSSION

● What does Paul mean when he says he wants to "know" Christ (Philippians 3:8, 10)? How does knowing Christ differ from knowing about Christ? How can we deepen our relationships with Christ?

● In Philippians 3:8, Paul states that everything that doesn't help him know Christ better is rubbish or trash. Do you think Paul gave up all of his personal goals? To what extent must we set aside our personal goals?

■ ■

APPLY■IT■TO
LIFE
THIS WEEK

The "Apply-It-To-Life This Week" handout (p. 62) helps people further explore the issues uncovered in today's class. Give everyone a photocopy of the handout. Encourage class members to take time during the coming week to explore the questions and activities listed on the handout.

TEACHER
TIP

If you didn't complete Option 2, substitute the eulogies from "My Eulogy" for the personal mission statements.

CLOSING

Purposeful Additions

(up to 10 minutes)

Keep people in their groups of four. Instruct group members to write on each other's personal mission statements one additional quality and challenge that would be good to include in that person's statement. For example, someone might write, "You're great with children. Maybe you could work with them regularly" or "With your imagination, you should try writing short stories." Encourage people to keep the suggestions specific and positive.

When everyone is finished, form a circle. Instruct people to place their papers on the floor and to join hands. Have adults pray silently, asking God for the wisdom to create statements that accurately reflect their true identities and challenge them to grow in Christ. After a minute or so, lead the class in praying aloud **Philippians 3:14** by using the following prayer or one like it. Say: **God, help me press on toward the goal to win the prize for which God has called me heavenward in Christ Jesus. Amen.**

 # For Extra Time

CIRCLE BLESSING
(up to 10 minutes)

Form a circle. Have class members take turns standing in the center of the circle. While each person is in the center of the circle, have the rest of the class tell that person how they've seen him or her grow in the past four weeks or name qualities or strengths that person already possesses that God could use in an even greater way.

NEW DIRECTIONS
(up to 10 minutes)

Form a circle (or multiple circles if your class is larger than eight). Ask everyone to respond to each of these statements:

- **One thing I'll remember about this course is...**
- **One lie about myself I've uncovered during this course is...**
- **One truth I've learned about myself during this course is...**
- **One thing I want to do as a result of this course is...**
- **One thing I'd tell a friend about this course is...**

Close with prayer, asking God to guide class members to realize their full potential in him.

From Here to Eternity

The Point: ▶ With God's help, we can live fulfilled, purposeful lives.
Scripture Focus: Philippians 3:7-14 and 2 Timothy 4:6-8

Reflecting on God's Word

Each day this week, read one of the following Scriptures and examine what it says about fulfilled, purposeful living. Then examine how well you are applying the message of the passage in your life. You may want to list your discoveries in the space under each passage.

Day 1: Genesis 12:1-9. God promises Abram land, descendants, and blessing.

Day 2: 1 Samuel 3:1-21. God calls the boy Samuel to be a prophet.

Day 3: 1 Samuel 17:1-58. David defeats the Philistine giant, Goliath.

Day 4: Esther 3–4. Esther risks her life to save her people.

Day 5: Judges 4–5. Deborah leads the Israelites to victory.

Day 6: Ruth 1–2. Ruth remains with and cares for Naomi.

Beyond Reflection

1. Buy or borrow the book *The Seven Habits of Highly Effective People* by Stephen Covey. This resource provides an in-depth look at creating personal purpose statements and helps you overcome obstacles you may encounter on your path to living an extraordinary life.

2. Ask a friend or another class member to become your accountability partner as you work to live out your true identity. Set a regular meeting time with your partner so you can encourage and help each other strive to fulfill your potentials in Christ.

Fellowship and Outreach Specials

Use the following activities any time you want. You can use them as part of (or in place of) your regular class activities, or you can plan a special event based on one or more of the ideas.

Book Study

To continue the personal growth begun in this course, ask class members to commit to be part of a study group. Work through the book *The Search for Significance* by Robert S. McGee or *The Seven Habits of Highly Effective People* by Stephen R. Covey. Both books have workbooks available. Contact your local bookstore for ordering information.

Apply-It-To-Life Together

Create a meeting based on the "Apply-It-To-Life This Week" handouts from the course. As a part of the meeting, ask volunteers to share what they discovered through each of the handouts. During the meeting, have class members choose at least two of the "Beyond Reflection" activities to do together. Set up a schedule with goals for the completion of each of the activities they choose.

Family Identity

Encourage class members who are married or have children to get together with their families to discuss how the principles they've learned can help them define who they are as a family. Encourage participants to create "family purpose statements" and to set goals for their families that support their purpose statements.

A Step Further

Invite a local Christian counselor or psychologist to speak to your class about the subject of self-identity. Before the seminar, brief the psychologist on the information you've already covered in this course.

Neighborhood Identity Groups

Have class members help you lead this course in a neighborhood setting to which they can invite their neighbors. Use the course as a springboard to talk about issues in people's lives and to share how Jesus can bring purpose and definition to life.

"Celebrate Life" Party

Help class members plan a huge celebration of life for the whole congregation. Have each person take part in the planning or leading of the event. Allow the class free rein to plan how they want the party to look and what events they want it to include. Encourage class members to make the party their own personal expression of life for the congregation.